How You Do Anything Is How You Do Everything

-A Workbook-

Original title:
The How You Do Anything Is How You Do Everything Workbook

Copyright 1988 by
Cheri Huber and June Shiver

ISBN: 0-9614754-1-2
Library of Congress Registration Number: TXU 346-109

Please direct correspondence to
A Center for the Practice of Zen Buddhist Meditation
P.O.Box 91   Mountain View, California   94042
or
Monastery/Interfaith Retreat Center
P.O.Box 1994 Murphys, California   95247

Dedicated to "Toughie"
beloved friend and teacher

Introduction

It is not possible to do this workbook wrong. This book is simply an opportunity for you to see a little more clearly how you are as a person, how you approach life, how you choose your values and beliefs, and this is not a realm in which right and wrong apply.

This workbook focuses on the "process" of you, not the particulars, the content of your life. What you do or believe or feel will not be the point; how you do it will be the point. If you observed how you do this workbook, you would probably learn more about who and how you are than you could learn from the content of the exercises. How you do anything is how you do everything.

For example, you might hold the belief that "life is sacred." A simple statement. This book will encourage you to explore how you know that. Who taught you to believe that? How does believing that affect your life? Does it help you in not suffering, or does it cause you to suffer? What happens if someone challenges that belief? Why do we have beliefs? What if it's not true? And so on... not to encourage you to do or not to do anything about your beliefs, but to encourage you to explore the whole process of believing and how believing affects you.

Life involves suffering. Here we define as suffering everything from displeasure or dissatisfaction to tragic loss or utter failure. The four causes of suffering:

1) not getting what you want
2) getting what you want and not being satisfied with it
3) having to endure the absense of those or that which you love
4) having to endure the presense of those or that which you do not love.

How we are and how we conduct our lives leads either toward suffering or away from suffering. Throughout this book you will be encouraged to see how you do what you do and asked to question whether your process causes you suffering or leads you away from it. This is the purpose of this workbook.

We are not suggesting that you make any decisions, just become aware. Notice everything. See if you can allow yourself to be exactly as you are with as few judgments as possible for the duration of this project. Of course, you will judge! See if you can become more interested in the process of judging than in what you are judging.

This book is for you. Your answers aren't going to be graded. You are you. Comparing yourself to anyone else is like comparing apples and oranges. No comparison is possible. And, of course, you will compare! Just see if you can become more interested in the process of comparing than in what is being compared.

Knowing how you are is the beginning of freedom, and it is true that looking inward, seeing ourselves, can be scary. If the opportunity arises, see if you can give yourself permission to be scared, resistant, angry, upset, frustrated, sad, and depressed as well as happy, excited, eager, open, and willing.

And please, if you decide to approach this workbook, do so with all the compassion for yourself that you can find. You are probably not a great artist or writer or psychologist or spiritual adept. So don't expect to draw like Leonardo DaVinci, write like Jane Austen, analyze like Carl Jung, or have insights like the Buddha.

Just be you.

In this workbook there are references to The Key (and the Name of the Key is Willingness), a book we wrote hoping perhaps to assist others in their spiritual practice. It is available through your local bookstore.

Draw a picture of life.

4.

What were the most important steps
    that brought you to where you are today?

In many of these exercises, your answers depend on "who" does the exercise. Each of us is made up of many different parts. Some people describe this as playing different roles, wearing different hats, or following different scripts. We are different ways at different times with different people. For instance, if your boss said, "There's something I need to talk to you about," you probably wouldn't respond the same way as if your best friend said the same thing. A different person takes a date to the movies on Sunday afternoon from the one who would watch a Sunday afternoon football game on TV with a bunch of old teammates from high school.

Many of us have similar "subpersonalities," a word we use to denote the various aspects of ourselves. Most of us have a part who judges us (the Judge), a Frightened Child, a Playful Child, perhaps an Athlete, a Perfectionist, a Lover, Daydreamer, Mother's Little Helper, Gossip, etc. We go in and out of these aspects constantly, and we have many common expressions that indicate the changes: "I'm not myself today," "Part of me wants to go but part of me doesn't," "I'm going to put myself on a diet." Even an emotional response like anger or sadness will be different with each of these people.

We have found it helpful to give these subpersonalities names, gentle, loving names even to the parts who seem not to have our best interests in mind. We'll often ask you to "name the part of you who..." in order to help you begin to get a sense of the movement between various facets of yourself.

Concerning this exercise:
Are you surprised at all by the order of the steps?
Did you leave any out?

6.

Draw a picture of yourself at work.

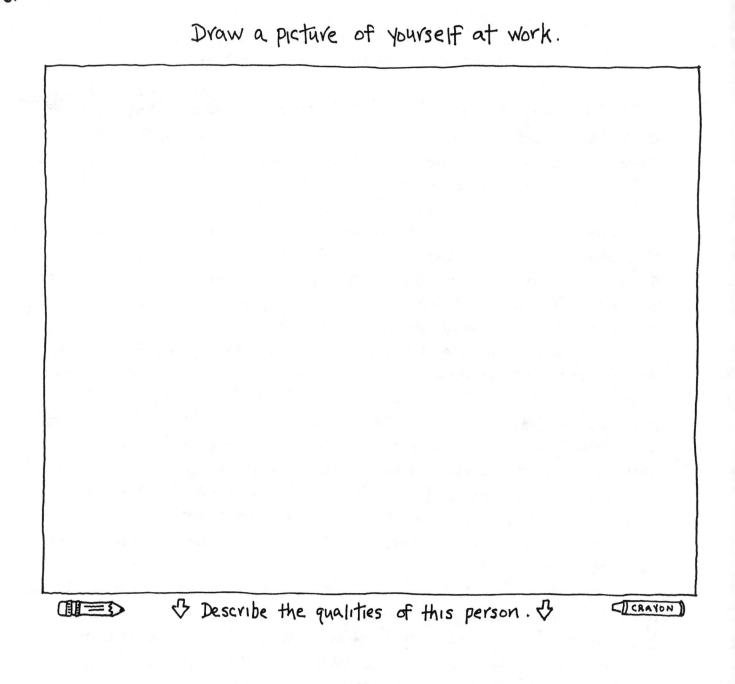

⇩ Describe the qualities of this person. ⇩   CRAYON

DRAW A PICTURE OF YOURSELF AT PLAY.
- Describe the qualities of this person-

8.

Draw a picture of yourself at home.

Describe the qualities of this person.

Where do you want to be in 5 years?

10 years?

15 years?

20 years?

What are you doing now that will lead to that?

What are you doing that will keep you from that?

Looking at yourself...

What I've been told about me...

What I tell myself about me...

What I really know about me...

This process can be applied to many topics.

What would make your life perfect?

Write a horoscope for yourself for the coming year.

14.

What happens to you when you feel uncomfortable?

How do you avoid discomfort?

What do you have in your life and what do you exclude from your life in order to avoid discomfort?

See if you can avoid the tendency to use your answers as an excuse to beat yourself up. Beating ourselves keeps us stuck. Beatings do not cause us to improve.

See if you can simply add an awareness of how you want your life to be and begin to notice how you stop yourself from having that.

Often it seems that just being aware isn't enough. We're very conditioned to believe that to have what we want in life requires that we get or do something. That desire to "do" keeps us stuck. When we see how we keep ourselves from having what we want and from being who we choose to be, we find that we already have everything we need and that we are inherently the person we choose to be.

Just watch.

When you see clearly what you're doing and how you're doing it, you'll also know why, and that it's not working, and you'll simply stop.

Trying to change keeps us stuck. See slearly and you have changed without even trying. And that change "works."

Think of something you want.

⇧ Write it down or draw it in here. ⇧

☆ What are you doing to get/have that? ☆

☆ What are you doing to get in your way? ☆

How are you when you get what you want?

How are you when you don't get what you want?

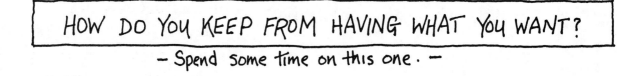

HOW DO YOU KEEP FROM HAVING WHAT YOU WANT?

— Spend some time on this one. —

What did you get
that you're not satisfied with
that's causing you to want
what you're wanting now?

The Four Causes of Suffering

- Not getting what you want

- Getting what you want and not being satisfied with it

- Having to endure the absence of those or that which you love

- Having to endure the presence of those or that which you do not love

SEE THE KEY, PAGES 20-23

When we find ourselves in circumstances we don't like our immediate assumption is that we need to change something, fix things somehow. Changing externals never resolves a problem. We all know the experience of disliking a job, a type of person, a certain atmosphere, etc., and leaving only to find ourselves in the same situation somewhere else.

When we look closely we usually see that the source of the difficulty comes down to wanting things not to be the way they are. We are afraid that if we accept them as they are, that very act will mean they won't change — they'll be that way forever and we'll be unhappy. There are actually several untrue assumptions operating:

1) I don't like it, therefore something is wrong with it.
2) As long as it's this way, I can't be happy (safe, content, etc.)
3) Resisting the way it is will cause it to change.
4) Accepting it means that it will always be that way and I'll be doomed to unhappiness.

We fail to see that resisting what is is the problem.

Our well-being is not dependent on any external. We think it is, but it is not. For instance: "I hate my job because my boss is a jerk." Now it's easy to think that that is a true statement and to believe:

1) I have to quit my job, or
2) I have to hang on, hating her/him and hoping s/he leaves, or
3) I have to go on and be willing to suffer until I can retire.

Not so. I also have the option of simply accepting the whole situation (boss included) exactly as it is.

The wonderful part is that at the moment we accept what is, it changes. The circumstances might or might not be the same. Our experience of them will be different.

List the ten things that are most important to you.

one	two
three	four
five	six
seven	eight
nine	ten

Let yourself recall a holiday.

Draw the experience, realistically and/or symbolically.

See yourself approaching the holidays...

What are you saying?	What are you doing?

What are you feeling?	What are you hoping for?

What are you afraid of?

You are having a very special person spend the holidays with you.

How would you like it to be?

If it doesn't happen that way, who in you will be disappointed?

How could you make it be the way you really want it to be?

26.

Write a dialogue between the part of you who likes holidays and the part who dislikes holidays. Can you name the parts?

What do you need to work on?

⇧ WRITE IT DOWN IN HERE. ⇧
⇩ FIVE QUESTIONS ⇩

1. How is this currently apparent in your life?

2. How has this been an ongoing process in your life?

3. What would you need to do to resolve it?

4. What are you willing to do to resolve it?

5. What are the pay-offs, positive and negative, for not resolving it?

+ POSITIVE +	− NEGATIVE −

(A gift)→ You can have anything in the world...

· What is it?

· How did you select it?

· What did you consider and not select?

· How will you feel having it?

· How will you be different?

· List the qualities of the gift you have selected. ⋈

Are these missing in your life currently?

Think of your most favorite and least favorite animal.

Write a story about them that uses the adjectives that show why you like and dislike each. (The gentle, kindhearted dog lifted her intelligent head and surveyed the sneaky, stupid...)

STRIPED
SKUNK

BLACK
BEAR

QUAIL

MOUNTAIN
LION

Can you own these qualities?

If money were no object...

Where would you go?

With whom would you go?

What would you do?

Think of the secrets you keep...

Who do you consider telling?

Who do you specifically not tell?

What/Who are you protecting?

⇨ What would people think if they knew? ⇦

Can you see how you feel these things about yourself, and can you be open to the possibility that others might not feel that way and don't have your values at all?

Think of a character from history, fiction or fantasy.
Write a story about this character in action.

Own the story as your story
and the character as a part of yourself.

Write a dialogue between you and the character.

Are you a compassionate person?

When are you most compassionate?

When are you least compassionate?

Are you more compassionate with yourself or others?

36.

What is the most loving, compassionate thing you could do for yourself right now?

What do you believe about yourself and life that keeps you from doing this?

WHO YOU ARE RIGHT NOW...

How do you feel? How old?	What do you think about life?
How would you change your life?	How would you change others?
What do you want?	What do you need?

Do this exercise regularly to get a sense of your changing selves.

What are your strengths

and weaknesses?

How do you know that's what they are? Who says so?

What do you <u>need</u> in order to be happy?

— Get picky with this one. Give details. Elaborate. Carry on at length. Draw pictures. Name names. —

What do you <u>really</u> need in order to be happy?

List the greatest moments in your life. Who (what part of you) was there?

Do this exercise with all the courage you can muster.
Be as fearless as possible.

I now give myself permission to...

Think of three dominant characteristics of someone you dislike.
Write them down.

1.

2.

3.

Think of three dominant characteristics of someone you like.
Write them down.

1.

2.

3.

Can you own those and see how you are like that, too?

44.

These are postures, attitudes, beliefs that you have learned and now cling to. Look to see how many of them bring happiness to your relationships and how many lead to unhappiness. Would you let go of them in order to have happy relationships?

SEE THE KEY, PAGES 38·39

What do other people expect from you?

They expect me to . . .

The standards by which we think others are judging us are the standards by which we are judging others.

This is what we call the "double reverse projection." I project onto you what I think about myself, and then I think you think it about me. I project my standards onto you and then believe you are judging me by my standards.

P.S. If the standards by which you are judging me are not the same as mine, it will never occur to me that you are judging me about those things!

At the end of the day,

review your day,

recall each interaction
throughout the day,

"...and then she said

describe each person
you encountered.

Remember what they were doing, how they were acting.

Can you see how you are that way?
Can you own those projections?

SEE THE KEY, PAGES 77-84

Imagine that you're going away.

What do you do?
What do you want others to do?

Imagine that someone else is going away.

What do you do?
What do you want them to do?

What book, song, and movie best describe your life?

What would you title a book, a song, and a movie about your life?

Tense yourself physically.

Relax.

Tense emotionally.

Relax.

Tense mentally.

Relax.

Repeat each exercise as you find out exactly where and how you do this.

Draw a picture of your body.

Move your attention
from the top of your head,

down through your entire body,

all the way to your toes,

and experience your body as fully as possible.

What kind of body is it?

How do you feel about it?

Is it comfortable to you?

How would you change it?

What do you value most?

What do you like most?

What do you dislike most?

Draw a picture of your feelings.

What does your drawing tell
you about how you see
yourself emotionally?

Which part of you drew your feelings?

What do you do to feel:

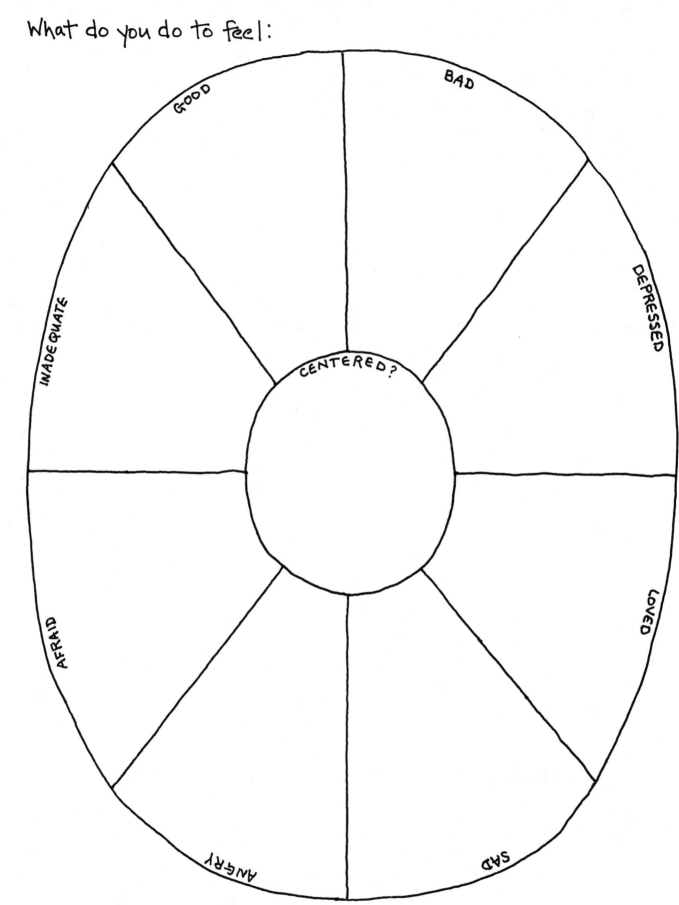

GOOD BAD

INADEQUATE DEPRESSED

CENTERED?

AFRAID LOVED

ANGRY SAD

Answer these quickly without "thinking."

• I'm happiest when

• Someday I'm going to

• When I'm really down, what I want to do is

• I feel anxious when

• I'm afraid that

• I like people who

• All it takes to make me happy is

• What I really want to do is

• I wish that

• I don't like people who

• A person really should

• I just hate it that

• I have everything I need, however

• If I could do whatever I wanted, I would

What makes you the saddest?

What might you do to take care of the part of you who feels the sadness?

When do you punish yourself?

How do you punish yourself?

When are you good to yourself?

How are you good to yourself?

What are you like when you're alone?

62.

What do you do to be good to someone or to take care of someone?

Will you do those things for you?

When do you feel defensive?

How do you defend yourself? What is your favorite defense?

What are you most insecure about?

How has this insecurity affected your life?

What makes you feel secure?

What do you trade for that security?

👉 Refer back to page 22

Reduce your list of ten
to the three things you consider most important.

1.

2.

3.

What would you like to:

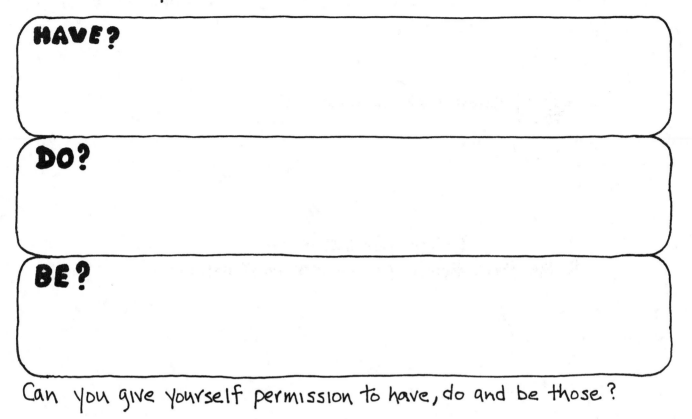

HAVE?

DO?

BE?

Can you give yourself permission to have, do and be those?

What stops you? How do you stop yourself?

How do you get disappointed?
(See if you can identify the <u>process</u> of disappointment.)

What do you expect or assume about your life
that causes you to be dissatisfied?
(Can you remember specific examples in which your assumptions and
expectations about life caused your dissatisfaction and suffering?)

How do you change when you're in a group? What does this change do for you?

How are you with someone you like ?

And with some one you dislike ?

Have you noticed that when you're with someone you like, you like yourself? And, of course, when you're with someone you dislike, not only do you dislike them, you dislike you, too?

It is also true that what we like about others are the things we like about ourselves, and what we dislike in others are the things we dislike in ourselves.

We like or dislike the way we _feel_ around others. Just for fun, the next time you're with someone you dislike, keep your attention focused on accepting, approving of, liking yourself and see what happens.

I'll allow myself:

* to love but not...

* to cry but not...

* to be angry but not...

* to play but not...

* to do what I want but not...

* to have what I want but not...

* to let go but not...

* to be loved but not...

* to feel good but not...

How have you changed in the last year?

How do you feel about the changes?

When did you first experience (recall the circumstances)

LOVE	ENVY
FEAR	ANXIETY
HATRED	COURAGE
GUILT	JEALOUSY
EMBARRASSMENT	JOY

When do you presently experience

LOVE	ENVY
FEAR	ANXIETY
HATRED	COURAGE
GUILT	JEALOUSY
EMBARRASSMENT	JOY

How old is the part of you who experiences

LOVE	ENVY
FEAR	ANXIETY
HATRED	COURAGE
GUILT	JEALOUSY
EMBARRASSMENT	JOY

Who in your life comes to mind when you consider

LOVE	ENVY
FEAR	ANXIETY
HATRED	COURAGE
GUILT	JEALOUSY
EMBARRASSMENT	JOY

Draw a picture of your mind.

CRAYON

What does the drawing tell you about how you see yourself mentally?

Which part of you drew your mind?

Complete the following:

I'm the kind of person who...

I'm the kind of person who...

I'm the kind of person who...

I'm the kind of person who...

Describe one thing about yourself that you wish were different.

Name the part of yourself who wants to be different.
What are her/his primary concerns?

We cannot experience anything other than our own experience. How would you know you wanted peace in your life, for example, if you didn't already know what peace feels like? When you're experiencing peace, it's coming from within you, you're "doing" peace. And this is true of anything else you might be "looking for." Love, happiness, contentment, well-being come from within.

Nothing external needs to change for you to have what you want. Example: Wealth is an attitude of mind. Rich is the ability to enjoy fully. Neither has anything to do with money or possessions. Many people have a lot of money but can't enjoy it because they're too worried about getting more or losing what they have.

So, if you've looking for something, do/be that. Also, don't waste your time chastising yourself for not doing it before now.

If you want to be happier – be happier.
If you want to be more relaxed – relax.
If you want more friends – be friendly.
Sounds simple.
It is.

The trouble with me is ... (Fill this space if you can.)

The good things about me are ... (Fill this space if you can.)

Which was easier to fill?

What are the three things you appreciate most about yourself?

 1.

 2.

3.

Draw a picture of yourself the way you like yourself least.
Describe the qualities of this person.

Who (which part of yourself) believes there's something wrong with you? Give her/him a name.

Describe the qualities of this part of yourself.

What is s/he afraid of?

What do you get out of maintaining this belief?

Write down three "positive" opinions.

1.

2.

3.

Write down three "negative" opinions.

1.

2.

3.

Explore each to determine the "pay-off" for maintaining it. What do you gain? What do you lose?

How do you determine what is positive and what is negative?

We assume that "positive" opinions are good for us. We've taught that we "should" have them, and yet when we look closely our positive opinions often lead to as much suffering as our "negative" ones. Many of the rules, standards, and beliefs that operate our daily lives have never been examined by us from an adult point of view. It's often helpful to examine not only <u>what</u> we do, but also <u>how</u> <u>we</u> <u>know</u> to do it.

Write down three things:

I believe
   1.

   2.

   3.

I think
   1.

   2.

   3.

I know
   1.

   2.

   3.

What difference do you experience in these?

When do you feel safe?

When do you feel unsafe?

Describe and/or draw the place where you feel safest.

Identify an issue.

```
┌─────────────────────────────────────────────────────┐
│                                                     │
│                                                     │
│                                                     │
│                                                     │
└─────────────────────────────────────────────────────┘
```

WRITE IT DOWN IN HERE ⬆

Jot down the beliefs you hold on to around this issue.

Jot down the beliefs you push away around this issue.

Can you name the parts of you who are on each side of this issue?

What we're asking you to explore in this exercise is how your belief systems and assumptions can conflict and therefore keep you stuck. For example, perhaps a part of you has been conditioned to believe: "If I keep working at it, I can pretty much arrange my life the way I want it to be." Another part, differently conditioned, might believe: "I don't have any real power. I'm just a pawn in this giant socio-political game and nothing I do makes any difference." The difficulty comes when we're not aware that different parts of us hold precisely opposite beliefs.

As we begin to pay attention to when opposing parts of ourselves are present, we can begin to see how they work to keep us right where we are, spinning our wheels, frustrated, and, often, puzzled.

One should...

I should...

People should...

You should...

We should...

They should...

Who said so?

Each of us has chosen a set of principles and values by which we live. There are things in our lives that are so in opposition to our principles and values that we cannot imagine them as options for ourselves. (By the way, it's good to explore these to be sure we really choose them and haven't simply been told they are true) However, most of what we hold on to and push away has little to do with ethics and morals and much to do with liking and disliking. Often we hold onto something that makes us miserable out of a sense of pride and identity. Expressions like "you can't teach an old dog new tricks" and "never give an inch" are examples. "I'm too old to change."; "I've always done it this way"; "This is just the way I am." Poor reasons.

These beliefs and others like them support your <u>idea</u> of who you are. If you look closely, you might see that you are paying too high a price just to keep this identity intact.

Give something new a try; you might prefer a new you.

Imagine the ideal you...

How does she/he look?	What are her/his qualities?
How is she/he different from you?	What would you have to give up to be the ideal you?

What is the best thing that could happen to you?

What is the worst thing that could happen to you?

I would be happy if only...

I wouldn't suffer if only...

My life would be perfect if only...

I wouldn't be angry if only...

My life would have been better if only...

I would have what I want if only...

I would be a better person if only...

Inside each of us is a "persistent voice of discontent." It talks in terms of <u>if onlies</u> and can never be satisfied. Its function is to keep you feeling as if there is always something missing, always something just beyond your reach, which, if only you could get to it, would finally bring you contentment.

What do you think would happen
if you stopped
believing this voice?

Create an "Add List."

Mention every good thing you can think of about
yourself
  -all that you do, love, enjoy, give, offer -
  -all good deeds and works, present and past-

My Add List

Hang up your add list
somewhere convenient.

Add something to it every day.

What was the nicest thing ever said about you?

What was the worst thing ever said about you?

What is the nicest thing you say about yourself?

What is the worst thing you say about yourself?

How do you give difficult information?

How do you hear difficult information most openly?

Imagine the ♡alentine you would like to receive.
— DRAW THE VALENTINE.—
Employ colors, paste, glitter, ribbon, flowers, chocolate, etc. if you'd like.

Draw a picture of your family.

What do you notice?

What do you appreciate most about the way you were raised?

What is your favorite childhood memory?

What does it tell you about who you are now?

List ☆ your ☆ father's

positive qualities   negative qualities

List ☆ your ☆ mother's

positive qualities   negative qualities

Watch to see how you exhibit each of these qualities in your life.

· · · · · ·If your mother were writing an in-depth description of you,
· · · · · ·? ·what would she say?

.... If your father were writing an in-depth description of you,
.... what would he say?

Remember,

these are your projections, your ideas about how someone sees you. Look carefully at what you've written and see how this is how the part of you who is like your mother sees you, and this is how the part of you who is like your father sees you.

The most important thing my
FATHER
ever told me was...

The most important thing my
MOTHER
ever told me was...

How did your mother maintain distance between herself and you?

How did your father maintain distance between himself and you?

How do you maintain distance between yourself and others?

★ What needs to be done? ★ How do you know it needs to be done? ★ Which part of you needs it? ★ How long have you known this needs to be done? ★ What are you doing toward getting it done? ★ How are you stopping yourself from getting it done? ★

Write a one-page definition of what a relationship is.

If you have people in your life who are willing to do this exercise, share your definitions. How are they similar? Different?

Picture yourself as you are in a relationship.

– WRITE AND/OR DRAW A DESCRIPTION. –

Picture yourself as you are not in a relationship.

- WRITE AND/OR DRAW A DESCRIPTION. -

How should a relationship be?
(LOOK CLOSELY. GIVE ALL THE DETAILS YOU CAN.)

List the major relationships in your life.

What are/were the hard places?

Which part of you does/did the relationship?

What needs are/were met?

In each one:

What do/did you learn?

What needs aren't/weren't met?

What patterns are you aware of?

How would the other person describe you?

What do you want in a relationship?

What won't you give?

What have you stopped risking?

My biggest problem in a relationship is...

What is your pay-off for having this problem?

What would you need to do to let go of it?

What stops you?

What do you say,
how do you act,
in order to get close to others?

What do you say,
how do you act,
in order to keep   others   away?

As you consider people in your life, past and present, are you sensing the patterns? It might seem quite accidental or coincidental that we seem always to wind up with the same kind of person, but it's not. Most of us have a very finely tuned sense of which people "fit" and which don't. It's important to keep in mind that we are each, in all our life situations, first and foremost, maintaining our identity.

However, that identity seems often not in accord with what I say I want. For instance, I complain about a lack of intimacy in my relationships but continue to pick people who are unavailable, uncommunicative, workaholics, etc. If I continue to make that same choice, it would be good to consider that perhaps it is I who am avoiding intimacy. I complain about being overweight but continue to choose eating over exercising; I complain about not having enough time to myself but continue to take on responsibilities.

As we explore the patterns and the pay-offs for having them, we get closer to the deeper identity we're protecting.

What are the "wedges" you most often use to avoid intimacy?

How do you use these wedges?

When do you use them?

How could you feel safe enough to let go of them?

Write a dialogue between:

     • the part of you who wants to be CLOSE
     • the part of you who wants to keep a d·i·s·t·a·n·c·e.

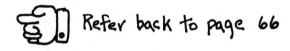 Refer back to page 66

Decide which is the most important
thing in your life.

[box]

How does this make you feel?

Review your life and make a list of commitments you have kept.
(We couldn't decide whether to leave a large space or a small space
for this answer.)

Which part of you

· makes commitments? _____

· keeps commitments? _____

· breaks commitments? _____

What have you wanted to commit to and continually found yourself unable to commit to?

MARRIAGE · CHILDREN · RELIGION

CHARITY · POLITICS · EDUCATION

What would you need to do in order to make that commitment?

What could you commit to at this time?

What would you expect in return?

What would you have to give up in order to have a relationship?

Create a new model for a relationship.

How would others respond to it? ✱

What would you have to give up to have it?

What would you have to allow yourself to have it?

Why don't you do it?

✱ Remember that what you project onto others is true for you and not necessarily true for them.

What are you looking for?

I am looking for...

Can you see ways in which what you're looking for is already present in your life?

How would you like your life to be?

In order to have that...

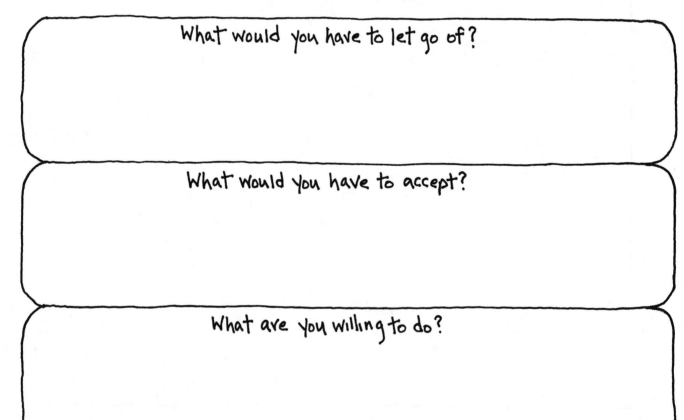

What would you have to let go of?

What would you have to accept?

What are you willing to do?

Write a dialogue between:

The part of you who is willing to change.

The part of you who is not willing to change.

You are going away for a long time alone...

What do you want to have with you?

Are there any surprises about what you forgot to list or the order in which you thought of things?

What could you "not live without"?

—WRITE AND/OR DRAW YOUR ANSWER.—

Consider the many different types of "goodbyes" in our lives.

Finish these sentences:

Saying goodbye is

Saying goodbye is

Saying goodbye is

Saying goodbye is

What does goodbye mean to you?

How do you say goodbye?

What do you feel with goodbyes?

How have goodbyes been in the past?

How could you take care of yourself through a goodbye?

What kinds of things help you with goodbyes?

 writing a letter?   reviving old memories?

giving a gift?   packing away old memories?

Something else?
How do these things help you?

Think of a person, situation, experience from your past that you can't seem to let go of. Write a "letter of closure" expressing everything you need to express in order to put this issue to rest.

Write a letter to forgive someone* you haven't yet forgiven.
(Attach pages if you letter grows long.)

* This someone can be inside of you, a part of yourself who did
something another part of you considers "unforgivable."

Even if someone or something no longer present is involved,

we can find resolution in ourselves

through acceptance and forgiveness.

Recall a time when you let go.

- WRITE AND/OR DRAW THAT EXPERIENCE. -

Describe your spiritual life.

-WRITE AND/OR DRAW YOUR ANSWER-

What does wisdom mean to you?

What is the wisest thing you've ever heard? How does this wisdom affect your life?

How could you be wise?

Draw a picture of your center.

What does your drawing tell you about how you experience yourself spiritually?

Which part of you drew your center?

Recall a time when you felt centered.

Centering...

What do you focus on?

What do you let go of?

Where is your attention?

What are you not paying attention to?

What happens with your
   body?

   feelings?

   mind?

From our center comes wisdom and compassion. Our center <u>is</u> wisdom and compassion. This is our higher Self, our True Nature, a more universal or cosmic identity. From center comes a sense of well-being, calm, peace, joy, comfort, and confidence. Life is no longer a question of I, me, mine versus you, yours — life is us and ours.

Coming from our center, we can see what is. Resistance falls away. Being here, now, present, accepting what is. No illusion of separateness. All.

Life is not a struggle, not a contest. Center is what's there when you stop doing everything else.

Life is. You are.

Those are not incompatible states.

Recall a time when you did something
you thought you couldn't do.

Look back over a difficult period and let yourself re-do it the way it would have been if you had known then what you know now.

Write yourself a letter of forgiveness for each incident.

Let yourself recall something you consider unfinished.

Would you like for it to be finished?

How could you finish it?

- WRITE AND/OR DRAW -

How much of life do you allow yourself to enjoy?

How do you keep yourself from enjoying your life?

Write a prescription for yourself that will heal a dis-ease
or discomfort you are currently suffering.

RX   DR. FEELGOOD
      1270 PEACEFUL ST.
      SERENITY, CA

Let an image come to you that represents the relationship between your body, feelings, mind, and center.

Draw the image.

What does this drawing convey to you?

Draw a picture of death.

If you knew you had only one month to live, how would you spend it? Would you live differently from now? Are there things you'd feel an urgency to do?

Are you afraid of dying? Of death?

Which parts would you talk about with a friend?

What would you not talk about?

Are there things you'd want to clear up with others before dying?

your life is a movie.

- Imagine the ending. Who will play you? What will your final line be? -

★ Think of one thing you'd like to do before you die. ★

⇩ ANSWER THESE QUESTIONS ⇩

How would it change you? How would you feel doing it? How would you feel having done it? Which part of you wants to do it? Which part of you stops you?

⇩

158.

You have lived your life and you are now very old.
Looking back over your life, what do you regret?

☞

Is there something you could do <u>now</u> to avoid that regret?
If so, write down the steps you're willing to take.

Where are you now in your life?

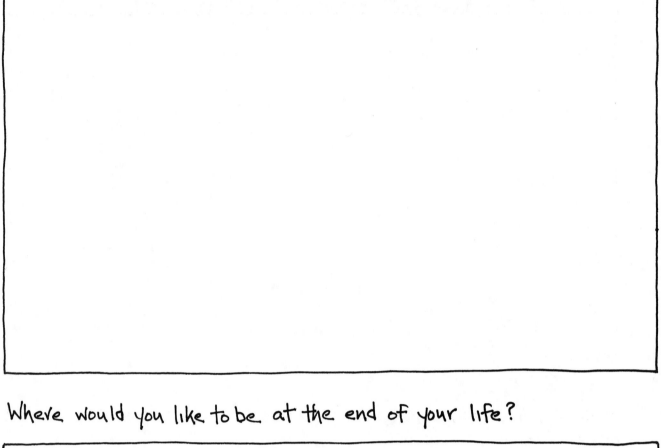

Where would you like to be at the end of your life?

Where will you be at the end of your life if you continue as you are now?

What do you need to let go of in order to be where you want to be at the end of your life?

How did you do this workbook?

Were there some exercises you skipped?

Were there some you jumped forward to?

Does looking at the exercises you skipped tell you anything about yourself?

What kinds of feelings came up as you contemplated the questions?

As you read each exercise, did you "judge" them in any way?

Are there some you're attracted to doing again?

Would you answer them differently?

Are there some you'd answer the same?

Did your answers ever surprise you?

"Who" did this workbook?

Did "different people" answer different questions?

How can you tell?

Can you appreciate yourself for having made this effort?

-NOTES-

— NOTES —

- NOTES -

- NOTES -

- NOTES -

-NOTES-

- NOTES -

- NOTES -